# FLIGHT of the GOLDEN PLOVER

## THE AMAZING MIGRATION BETWEEN HAWAII AND ALASKA

STORY BY DEBBIE S. MILLER

ILLUSTRATIONS BY DANIEL VAN ZYLE

UNIVERSITY OF ALASKA PRESS

FAIRBANKS

DEDICATIONS

*For Robin and Casey, and for children who dream of flight and marvel at the migrations of birds.*
—D. S. M.

*To Mum, who gave me my love for the pencil and the great outdoors. To Granny, who let me climb trees.*
—D. V. Z.

ACKNOWLEDGMENTS

I'm grateful to many people who helped create this book. A special thanks to Wally and Patricia Johnson, who shared their knowledge about the Pacific golden plover, guided me across the tundra, and answered countless questions. Thanks to Kay Hackney, Fred DeCicco, and Luke for sharing their home in Nome; Phil Bruner, Philip Martin, Brian McCaffery, Peter Connors, Dan Gibson, Pam Bruce, Kate Moitoret, and Robin Miller for reviewing the manuscript and making suggestions; editor Marlene Blessing for falling in love with a bird she had never seen; Ellen Wheat and Carolyn Smith for their meticulous editing; and Dan Van Zyle, whose love for the golden plover and other wildlife shines through his pictures. A special thanks to my family for sharing the world of the golden plover with me. Last, thanks to the Alaska State Council on the Arts for their travel support, and the Fairbanks SCBWI writers group for critiquing the manuscript. Without the help and talents of many, this book would not be. —D. S. M.

I thank Roslyn, my wife and partner, the light of my life, for being there through thick and thin. My sincere gratitude to Debbie Miller, whose fascination with a little seven-ounce bird created a saga that moved my heart to become a child again; to Marlene Blessing, Ellen Wheat, and Betty Watson, whose guidance, passion, and expertise were essential to an exciting and creative collaboration; and thanks also to my midnight counsel, brother Jon. —D. V. Z.

Library of Congress Cataloging-in-Publication Data

Miller, Debbie S.
 Flight of the golden plover : the amazing migration between Hawaii and Alaska / story by Debbie S. Miller ; illustrations by Daniel Van Zyle. — [Rev. ed.]
    p. cm.
 Originally published: Anchorage : Alaska Northwest Books, c1996.
 ISBN 978-1-60223-151-1 (pbk. : alk. paper)
1. Pacific golden plover—Hawaii—Juvenile literature. 2. Pacific golden plover—Alaska—Juvenile literature. 3. Pacific golden plover—Migration—Hawaii—Juvenile literature.
4. Pacific golden plover—Migration—Alaska—Juvenile literature. I. Van Zyle, Daniel, ill. II. Title.
 QL696.C43M55 2011
 333.95'833—dc22

                  2011004424

Designer: Elizabeth Watson

University of Alaska Press
P.O. Box 756240
Fairbanks, AK  99775-6240

Printed by Samhwa Printing Co., Ltd., Seoul, Korea through Alaska Print Brokers, Anchorage, Alaska.
                  March 2011

**Pronunciation guide**
For Hawaiian words:
  kōlea (ko-LAY-ah)
  Kumukahi (koo-moo-KA-hi)
  Haleakalā (ha-lee-ah-ka-LA)
  nēnē (nay-nay)
For Eskimo words:
  tuusiik (too-zeek)
  tullik (tool-lick)

# The Annual Migration Route of the Pacific Golden Plover Between Hawaii and Alaska

Long ago, the Hawaiian people believed that many gods appeared as spirit beings through birds and other animals. The golden plover, known as kōlea, was a powerful bird mentioned in hula chants and legends. Kōlea often embodied the spirit of Kumukahi, a god with strong healing powers.

Some people think that the golden plover helped ancient Polynesian explorers to discover the Hawaiian Islands. These seafaring people may have followed flocks of plovers in the hope of finding distant lands.

Each year these birds fly thousands of miles across the Pacific, making one of the greatest oceanic migrations on earth. This is the story of the Pacific golden plover's amazing journey between Hawaii and Alaska, and its life in two special, very different places.

Twinkling stars fade above the ocean. The dawn sky grows soft and pink. An incoming tide hisses across the shore. A golden plover ruffles his feathers, shaking off beads of sea spray onto a jumble of lava rocks.

The plover greets the day with other roosting plovers near Haleakalā, one of the largest volcanoes in the world. Here, on the Hawaiian island of Maui, this shorebird lives most of the year.

A few quick steps, a whisper of feathers, and the plover pumps his wings rapidly. Through the quiet morning air, he flies above rolling hills, across rivers of lava that once bubbled and sizzled down the volcano to the sea.

A fast flier, the plover soon reaches a grassy slope. This is his territory, a place where he returns each year to feed on grasshoppers and other insects. The Hawaiian goose, nēnē, browses nearby, but there are no other plovers. This plover has established his territory and chased away any plovers that have challenged him for the site.

The plover dashes forward, then freezes, as still as a statue. Spotting movement in the grass, he quickly jabs his beak at the ground and catches a grasshopper. While he swallows his food, the first rays of sunlight paint his feathers gold, as though the dawn glowed from within him.

It is late April, and the plover has just finished growing his colorful breeding plumage. He looks striking and regal with his velvet black breast, distinctive white stripe above his eye and down his neck, and golden-flecked back. With new flight feathers he is ready for the long northern journey to Alaska, a distant, great wilderness with plenty of nesting space and countless insects for food.

The plover is prepared for the incredible nonstop migration over the Pacific Ocean. For the past month he has increased his feeding, building up reserves for the 3,000-mile flight. His weight has doubled since autumn. About one-third of the plover's body is fat, which will provide energy for his long trip. Late that day, he leaves Haleakalā and joins a flock of plovers feeding along the coast.

As the sun sinks into the ocean, the wet sand turns to liquid gold. Plovers and ruddy turnstones scurry along the water's edge, prowling the tide pools for food. The plover snatches a few small hermit crabs, his last meal before the big flight.

Sky and sea grow darker. The plover pauses and looks north at the distant clear horizon. It is time to begin the migration.

*Chalee . . . chalee . . . chalee,* the plover calls as he takes off. Immediately, the other plovers answer *chalee* and follow. The flock ascends in circles, climbing several thousand feet, as though they are flying up an invisible spiral staircase into the twilight.

High in the sky, the plover feels the strong southern wind that will help push the flock northward. He points his beak toward Alaska and pumps his wings steadily through the starry sky. The night sky is like a giant road map for plovers and other migratory birds. They use the position of the stars and sun to guide them to their home ranges. For two days the flock flies thousands of feet above the ocean, through light and darkness, without stopping to rest or feed.

Their muscular breast, powerful wings, hollow bones, and streamlined body enable these shorebirds to make one of the world's longest over-water migrations. Bird lungs can absorb more oxygen than those of other animals, an adaptation that allows plovers to fly at high altitudes. By taking advantage of the best wind conditions, plovers can travel an average speed of sixty miles per hour.

As the plover nears the Alaska coast, the winds blow harder and the clouds grow thick and dark. He presses on through a swirling mist. Gradually the drizzle turns to rain and sleet, then snow. Some of the birds become separated from the flock. The plover continues, beating his wings through the snow-laced sky.

Suddenly, the gray outline of land comes into view. The plover and other birds from the flock alight on the frozen tundra of a remote, windswept island. When these strong fliers left Hawaii it was eighty degrees Fahrenheit. Now they feel the chill of winds off the ice-choked Bering Sea with temperatures near freezing. To keep warm, the plover fluffs his feathers, creating air pockets that insulate him. His layer of body fat also helps him combat the cold. In the gusting wind and snow, he stops to nibble on some old crowberries— his first food in two days. Nearby, a herd of musk oxen grazes with snow-frosted faces. Their shaggy skirts of fur ripple in the wind.

The next day the skies are clear. The plover takes off again, heading toward the same peninsula of land where he has nested for the past few years. He soon recognizes familiar shorelines, creeks, and valleys, tundra slopes, scattered villages, and mountains. He is almost there.

At last the golden plover reaches a distinct patch of rock-studded tundra, his nesting ground. Snow partially covers the treeless slopes that surround him. He looks out across miles of open land toward the distant Bering Sea. The brisk air is filled with the lilting song of the Lapland longspur, the piping of sandpipers, and the gargling calls of the sandhill cranes. Birds are arriving in Alaska's vast open spaces from all corners of the earth.

The plover proclaims his breeding territory and sets out to attract a mate. He takes off, fluttering his wings rapidly to gain altitude. As he levels off, he beats his wings slowly and calls *pee-chu-wee, pee-chu-wee, pee-chu-wee* above his territory. It sounds as though he is announcing *I-am-here, I-am-here, I-am-here!* With wings stiffly outstretched, he glides downward, then flutters up again, repeating his display and calls. This "butterfly flight" ends when he gradually loses elevation and glides gently to the ground.

Within a few days, a female plover joins him, having just completed her migration. The male searches for an ideal nesting spot and begins the scraping ritual. He proposes several nesting sites to the female. At each spot, he scrapes the ground until he creates a shallow bowl in the earth. Then, stepping in front of the site, he displays his underfeathers to the female. When she approves of one nesting site, she nudges the male and sits on the spot.

The male then gathers lichen and tiny leaves for the nest, which blends in perfectly with the dry tundra slope. The pair mates. Soon the female lays four buff-colored, brown-spotted eggs. She arranges them to point toward the center of the nest like the petals of a flower.

Both the male and female tend the nest. The male usually sits on the nest during the early part of the day. Later the female takes her turn warming the eggs. When not on the nest, they spend their time eating insects. Here in northern Alaska there is no darkness during the summer, so birds can feed around the clock.

One morning while the male tends the nest, he spots something moving in the willow bushes. Alarmed, he scurries away from the nest, crying *leee … leee … leee.* Out of the bushes trots an arctic fox, a feared predator that often raids the nests of birds.

The fox sniffs the ground, then moves closer to the nest. Quickly, the plover drags one wing on the ground and cries as though injured, luring the fox away from the eggs. The plover flies a short distance, then continues to drag his wing. This "broken wing dance" successfully tricks the fox, which wanders off across the tundra in search of other prey. The male soon returns to his safe nest.

*Tap, tap, tap.* After three weeks, the chicks begin pecking at their shells. Their protective parents stand by the nest, waiting for the chicks to hatch. One by one, the tiny wet birds emerge from the cracked eggs. The sun and wind dry their downy gold and brown-mottled feathers which blend in well with the ground and conceal the chicks from predators.

The tundra hums and buzzes with insects on this warm June day. When only a few hours old, the little chicks boldly leave their nest. On spindly legs, they wobble through the grasses and bright tundra wildflowers. The chicks instinctively peck, snatch, and gobble the endless supply of mosquitoes, flies, and bugs. Unlike chicks of other birds whose parents feed them, these newborn plovers feed themselves soon after hatching. For the first few days of their lives, the chicks return to the nest to be warmed by their parents.

In the early weeks, the parents watch over their young so that predators won't harm them. Yet one day, a chick wanders from the nest. As often happens, a jaeger is flying nearby, searching the tundra for a meal. Its keen eyes quickly spot the chick's movement. The jaeger hovers for a few seconds, then suddenly dives and snatches the chick in its powerful beak. Distress cries of the chick's parents pierce the air.

During the nesting season, hungry predators and fierce arctic storms can destroy many clutches of eggs and claim the lives of many chicks.

The three remaining chicks grow rapidly. In July, when the birds are about one month old, they are ready to fly and survive without their parents' protection. The fledglings try out their newly feathered wings. One young female, slightly smaller than her siblings, has a difficult time learning to fly. She awkwardly flaps her wings and bounces across the tundra, trying to become airborne.

By August, the parents have grown fat once again and are ready to migrate south. They, and other adult plovers, take off, climbing high in the sky to find favorable wind currents. They follow the coastline that points them toward Hawaii. Meanwhile, the young fledglings stay on the tundra to feed and gain strength so they can begin their first migration. It is unlikely they will see their parents again.

Within a few weeks, the fledglings are stronger. Without any adult leaders, flocks of young plovers begin to fly south. These three-month-old birds have inherited the amazing instinct to find their island wintering grounds across thousands of miles of ocean.

The young plovers wing their way across a patchwork of bright autumn colors, over herds of musk oxen and caribou, wandering grizzly bears and wolves. Their wings swiftly carry them to the last fringe of golden tundra that meets the endless sea.

With the coming of Alaska's winter, they cannot turn back. At dusk, the young fliers set out across the Pacific Ocean. Like their parents, the plovers climb thousands of feet above the water to ride the winds.

In the beginning, these plovers experience the best of flight conditions. A full moon casts a soft light in the night sky, and a strong seasonal wind pushes them toward the distant islands. Hour after hour they fly on the path of the wind toward a new home.

But, as night falls on the second day, the wind shifts. The birds use all their pumping strength just to stay on route. Weaker birds are blown off course, and some exhausted birds die at sea.

The young female, who only weeks ago was just learning to fly, has come thousands of miles. Now she grows weary as she beats her wings through the pressing wind. With only a few miles remaining on her journey, she suddenly feels turbulent storm clouds around her. The whirl of updrafts and downdrafts tosses and bounces her above the ocean. Heavy raindrops pelt her feathers. Wet and exhausted, she descends through the storm clouds.

As she nears the churning sea, a strange ghostly light appears through the curtain of rain. Above the whitecaps, her wet wings push her toward the light. She soon hears the familiar sound of waves crashing upon the shore. Her sharp eyes pick out the moonlit outline of a lighthouse and a rocky point. She has reached the Hawaiian Islands!

In the lee of the lighthouse, the exhausted plover rests. By dawn, the storm passes and the first rays of sunshine warm the plover's golden-flecked back. There, on the grassy slopes that sweep to the sea, the young plover will find her new winter home.

# FACTS ABOUT THE PACIFIC GOLDEN PLOVER

**SCIENTIFIC NAME:** *Pluvialis fulva.*
**COMMON NAME:** Pacific golden plover. The name plover comes from a French word meaning "the rain bird." In Europe, flocks of migratory plovers historically arrived at the beginning of the autumn rainy season.
**HAWAIIAN NAME:** *Kōlea,* meaning "one who takes and leaves."
**ALASKA NAME:** Eskimo people often named birds by the sound of their calls. *Tuusiik* is a Central Yupik name; Inupiat people call the plover *tullik.*
**DESCRIPTION:** Shorebird. Long legs, short tail, sharply pointed wings, dove-like head, short bill, muscular breast, streamlined body.
**HEIGHT:** 11 inches.

**WINGSPAN:** About 2 feet.
**WEIGHT:** Chicks weigh about as much as 5 nickels (25 grams, less than 1 ounce). Adult plovers double their body weight just before migration, and can weigh as much as a medium-size apple (200 grams, about 7 ounces).
**PLUMAGE:** Males have striking colors during breeding season. Black belly, white stripe extending from above eye and down neck, with a black, white, and gold-speckled back. Females have a lighter, mottled appearance. Males and females molt (grow new feathers) before the spring migration and after the fall migration.
**RANGE AND HABITAT:** Breeds in Western Alaska and Siberia along the coast. Winters in Hawaii and in places throughout the South Pacific and Indian Oceans. Occasionally found on the west coast of California. Plovers choose grassy areas with a good insect supply for their habitat. In Hawaii they are commonly seen on lawns, golf courses, and fields. In Alaska they prefer dry upland tundra slopes. They also feed and gather together in coastal areas.

**FOOD:** Feeds on insects, crustaceans and other invertebrates, and berries.
**BEHAVIOR:** Swift flyer. Runs short distances then stops when feeding. Males often return to the same nesting site each year. Many plovers establish individual territories on their winter range; a territory is about the size of a football field. Young birds are less territorial and often flock together. Golden plovers commonly roost together on winter range for protection against predators.
**NESTING HABITS:** Builds ground nests of lichens and leaves that blend perfectly with the tundra. Commonly lays four eggs that hatch in 23 to 24 days. Both parents tend the nest.
**PREDATORS: Hawaii**—feral cats and owls. **Alaska**—arctic foxes, parasitic jaegers, and other raptors.
**MIGRATION:** The 3,000-mile non-stop migration between Hawaii and Alaska takes about two days. Average flight speed is approximately 60 mph. Altitude unknown, but could range from 10,000 to 20,000 feet above the ocean.

**NAVIGATION:** Golden plovers and other migratory birds use the stars and the sun's position to guide them. Plovers may also orient themselves to the magnetic fields of the earth.
**LIFE SPAN:** Possibly 20 years.